The Power of

Excerpts from *If*

Mark Batterson

BakerBooks

a division of Baker Publishing Group
Grand Rapids, Michigan

© 2015 by Mark Batterson

Published by Baker Books
a division of Baker Publishing Group
P.O. Box 6287, Grand Rapids, MI 49516-6287
www.bakerbooks.com

This book is excerpted from *If*, published in 2015.

Printed in the United States of America

ISBN 978-0-8010-1906-7

Unless otherwise indicated, Scripture quotations are from the Holy Bible, New International Version®. NIV®. Copyright © 1973, 1978, 1984, 2011 by Biblica, Inc.™ Used by permission of Zondervan. All rights reserved worldwide. www.zondervan .com

Scripture quotations labeled KJV are from the King James Version of the Bible.

The Proprietors are represented by Fedd & Company, Inc.

In keeping with biblical principles of creation stewardship, Baker Publishing Group advocates the responsible use of our natural resources. As a member of the Green Press Initiative, our company uses recycled paper when possible. The text paper of this book is composed in part of post-consumer waste.

15 16 17 18 19 20 21   7 6 5 4 3 2 1

Contents

1. The Power of *If*   5
2. Who If   14
3. Bold Predictions   23
4. I Dwell in Possibility   31
5. Change Agents   40
6. One Last *If*   50

   Notes   57

1

The Power of *If*

✔ Kiss my wife on top of the Eiffel Tower.

It was a picture perfect day in Paris. After climbing 669 steps to the second floor, we hitched a very scary elevator ride to the top of the Eiffel Tower. Then, with France as my witness, I kissed my wife. Life goal #102? Check!

And it all started with *if*.

I'll explain, but first, let's have a little fun. How was that goal accomplished? Well, that depends on how you look at it. You could simply say that I puckered my lips, took an approach path from the left, closed my eyes at the last second, and voilá—a kiss in France, not to be confused with a French kiss.

That's how it happened, but there's more to it than that. That simple kiss was the result of a rather complex itinerary. We flew out of Dulles International Airport on an Airbus A320, made it through French customs, took the regional RER train to Paris, hailed a taxi whose driver enjoyed saying *mademoiselle* a little too much for my taste, and got walking directions from a French lady with a dog in her purse. Not even kidding! Classic as a croissant! But that too is just a fraction of the story.

You could argue that our Eiffel Tower kiss originated the moment I set life goal #102. And that's partially true. You won't accomplish 100 percent of the goals you don't set. But the true origin of our kiss traces all the way back to the 1889 World's Fair in Paris when more than a hundred artists submitted plans to design the centerpiece, the masterpiece of the Exposition Universelle.

The winner was an engineer named Alexandre Gustave Eiffel, who proposed a 984-foot tower, the tallest building in the world at that time. Skeptics scoffed at his design, calling it useless and artless. Eiffel called her *La Dame De Fer*—the Iron Lady.

It was Gustave Eiffel's *if* that made our romantic rendezvous atop the tower possible, but Eiffel himself thanked seventy-two scientists, engineers, and mathematicians on whose shoulders he stood. Their names are inscribed on the tower, and without their collective genius, our kiss is cancelled. So I guess we owe our kiss to each of their *ifs* as well.

Then there are the three hundred riveters, hammermen, and carpenters who put together the 18,038-piece jigsaw puzzle of wrought iron in two years, two months, and five days. Oh, and don't forget the acrobatic team Eiffel hired to help his workers maintain balance on very thin beams during strong gusts of wind. We have each of them to thank—as well as the Paris city council that voted in 1909 *not* to tear down the tower despite the fact that its twenty-year permit had expired. We owe our kiss to each councilmember and to each of the voters who put them in office.

It's starting to sound like all of history revolves around and conspired for our kiss, so let me stop there and make my point. Every moment, like our kiss atop the Eiffel Tower, is created by millions of *ifs* that combine in a million different ways to make that moment possible.

And if you need to read that sentence again, no shame. It's complicated—as complicated as the sovereignty of God. Yet as simple as *if*.

Gustave Eiffel did not build his tower so Lora and I could kiss on top of it. Nevertheless, his *if* made it possible. And it's your *ifs* that open doors of opportunity for others, most of whom you won't meet on this side of eternity. But make no mistake about it, every little *if* makes an exponential difference across time and eternity.

History is like an intricately interwoven tapestry with infinite patterns that only the Omniscient One can see and foresee—but *if* threads the needle. Your *ifs* don't just change the trajectory of your life; they change the course of history.

Our kiss atop the Eiffel Tower is part of a chain reaction that started when I wondered if Lora would go out with me. Then I acted on that *if*—well, actually I dialed and hung up a few times first. You could get away with that before caller ID.

Long story short, one *if* led to another *if*, which led to *I do*. The net result? Twenty-two years of marriage and three *ifs* named Parker, Summer, and Josiah.

If you stop and think about it, everything begins with *if.*

Every achievement, from the Nobel Prize to the Oscars, begins with *what if?* Every dream, from landing a man on the moon to the moon pies created to commemorate it, begins with *what if?* Every breakthrough, from the internet to iTunes, begins with *what if?*

There are 1,784 *ifs* in the Bible. Most of those *ifs* function as conditional conjunctions on the front end of God's promises. If we meet the condition, God delivers on the promise! So all that stands between your current circumstances and your wildest dreams is one little *if.*

One little *if* can change everything.

One little *if* can change anything.

WHAT IF?

On August 15, 1987, Howard Schultz was faced with the toughest decision of his life—whether or not to buy a small chain of coffeehouses with a strange name: Starbucks.

Knowing what we know now, it seems like a no-brainer. But to Schultz, the $3.8 million price tag felt like a case of the salmon swallowing the whale. In his memoir, *Pour Your Heart into It*, the architect behind the Starbucks brand reflects on his *what if* moment.

> *This is my moment*, I thought. *If I don't seize the opportunity, if I don't step out of my comfort zone and risk it all, if I let too much time tick on, my moment will pass.* I knew that if I didn't take advantage of this opportunity, I would replay it in my mind for my whole life, wondering: *What if?*[1]

Howard Schultz made a defining decision to give up the safety net of his $75,000 salary to pursue his passion for all things coffee. Starbucks stock went public five years later, on June 26, 1992. It was the second most actively traded stock on the NASDAQ that day, and by the closing bell its market capitalization stood at $273 million. Not bad for a $3.8 million investment!

Starbucks now has 16,580 stores in 40 countries, with revenues topping $4.7 billion, and their 137,000 employees totals twice the population of Greenland. By conservative estimates, Starbucks sold 3,861,778,846 cups of coffee last year.[2] Not to mention the other 87,000 possible drink combinations![3]

And every sip of every drink started with *what if*.

For the record, my favorite drink at Starbucks is a caramel macchiato. Just because we own and operate an independent coffeehouse on Capitol Hill doesn't mean I'm antiestablishment. Listen, if I'm nowhere near Ebenezer's coffeehouse, I'll take caffeine wherever I can get it. Which, thanks to Starbucks, seems like every other street corner in America!

If you reverse engineer Starbucks all the way back to its humble origins, it started with Howard Schultz's *what if*. That's true of Ebenezer's too—*what if* we built a coffeehouse where our church and our community could cross paths?

A million customers later, that *what if* is making lots of dreams come true. Every penny of net profit, more than $1 million now, has been reinvested in a wide variety of kingdom causes. And every penny traces back to *what if*.

What's your *what if*?

If you don't know yet, keep reading.

COUNTERFACTUAL THINKING

Technically, history is the study of past events—what actually happened. But there is a branch of history, counterfactual theory, that asks the *what if* questions. It considers the alternate realities that might have emerged if the hinges of history had swung the other way.

It's been said that *what if* is the historian's favorite question.[4]

What if one of the four musket balls that passed through George Washington's coat during the Battle of Monongahela in 1755 had pierced his heart?

What if the D-Day invasion by Allied forces on June 6, 1944, had failed to halt the Nazi regime?

What if the confederates had won the Battle of Little Round Top at Gettysburg on July 2, 1863?

History is full of *what ifs*, and so is Scripture.

What if David had missed Goliath's forehead?

What if Esther had not fasted, thereby finding favor, thus saving the Jewish people from genocide?

What if Joseph and Mary had not heeded the angel's warning to flee Bethlehem before Herod's henchmen showed up?

Let's stay in that vein.

Counterfactual theory is simply an exercise in counterfactual thinking. And it's not just a helpful exercise for historians; it's a healthy exercise for anyone and everyone. Counterfactual thinking is a critical dimension of goal setting and decision making. It's thinking outside the box. It's going against the grain. It's the divergent ability to reimagine alternatives.

And that's what this little book is designed to do. It's not just history or Scripture that are full of *what if* moments. They are the turning points, the tipping points in our lives too!

I recently spent two days with a life coach crafting a life plan.

I went through nineteen exercises with my life coach, each one aimed at reimagining my life. The focus was my future, but we looked at it through the prism of my past. It was like a connect-the-dots puzzle, with the letters spelling out God's faithfulness.

By the time we were done, my sense of destiny was off the charts. One of those exercises involved storyboarding my life by identifying turning points. Next, we titled the chapters of my life. Finally, we pinpointed what are called "life gates"—the defining moments that change the trajectory of our lives. They are the *what if* moments when a dream is conceived, a decision is made, or a risk is taken.

Those two days will pay dividends for the rest of my life. I only wish I hadn't waited as long as I did to do it. Honestly, I'd spent more time planning vacations than planning my life! I had some life goals, like goal #102. But I wasn't living with the kind of intentionality it takes to turn possibilities into realities.

What are the *what if* moments in your life?

If you can't identify any in your past, it's time to create some in your present.

2

Who If

Every *what if* is created twice.

The first creation is an idea that is conceived in the mind, the heart, the spirit. The second creation is the physical manifestation of that *what if*, whatever it is. Some *what ifs* take blueprints plus brick and mortar. Others require a keyboard, a camera, or a chef's kitchen.

But no matter what it is, everything that exists was once an idea in someone's mind. Before becoming a physical reality, it was nothing more than an electro-chemical signal firing across synapses deep within the cerebral cortex.

Let me use Washington, DC, as exhibit A.

The map of our capital city was first conceived in the mind of a French-born architect and engineer named Pierre Charles L'Enfant. He was commissioned by George Washington to survey a ten-mile square that was largely farmland and swampland. Even a decade later, the population of the capital city was only 8,144 at its first official census. While surveying, L'Enfant did spot one topographical feature, Jenkins Hill, that he thought held promise for what he called Congress House.

That's the hill where I've lived and pastored for nearly two decades—Capitol Hill.

After surveying the land, L'Enfant transferred his ideas onto a twenty-ounce piece of paper that was handed to President George Washington on August 19, 1791. That original map now sits enshrined in a 108-pound Plexiglas case breathing pressurized argon gas at the Library of Congress.

For more than two centuries, the L'Enfant Plan has framed the cityscape of Washington, DC. It has taken trillions of dollars; tons of marble, brick, and concrete; and countless hours of manual labor for that *what if* to become reality. But the reality is, whether I'm driving down Pennsylvania Avenue, rounding Dupont Circle, or even running on the National Mall, I'm navigating the map that L'Enfant dreamed up. My physical reality was once an idea in the mind of Pierre Charles L'Enfant.

That's true of everything, even you. The psalmist said it best:

> For you created my inmost being;
> > you knit me together in my mother's
> > > womb.
> I praise you because I am fearfully and won-
> derfully made;
> > your works are wonderful,
> > I know that full well.
> My frame was not hidden from you
> > when I was made in the secret place,
> > when I was woven together in the depths
> > > of the earth.
> Your eyes saw my unformed body;
> > all the days ordained for me were written
> > in your book
> > before one of them came to be.[1]

You were once an idea in the mind of almighty God. And God only has good ideas! You are the physical manifestation of God's eternal plans and purposes. Simply put, you are God's *what if*. And just as God created you, you are called to create.

Just five words into Genesis, God creates the heavens and the earth. It's the first revelation of God's character. Then, when you get to the next to last chapter of Revelation, God is creating a new heaven and a new earth. From start to finish, God never stops creating.

It's who He is. It's what He does. And we are most like Him when we exercise our creative capacity to *what if*.

ONE GOD IDEA

I'd rather have one God idea than a thousand good ideas.

Good ideas are good, don't get me wrong. But it's God ideas that change the course of history. Simply put, a God idea is an idea that doesn't originate with you. It's the divine *what if*. They often start out as fleeting thoughts or crazy ideas. But it's those ideas that put God's glory on display.

Ebenezer's coffeehouse has had more than a million customers, but it was once a crazy idea that fired across my synapses: *This crack house would make a great coffeehouse*. I knew that idea was either a God idea or a bad idea. It's often tough to discern the difference, but the only way to find out is to give it a go.

After hosting a Convoy of Hope outreach at DC's RFK stadium for ten thousand people, I heard the Holy Spirit whisper, *Now I want you to do this every day!*

It took an entire year to plan for and pull off that outreach, so the idea of doing it every day seemed crazy! But by definition, a God-ordained dream is beyond your ability to pull off. That was the genesis of our Dream Center in DC.

Every book I've written was once a *what if*, including *If*.

The Circle Maker was my first book to hit the *New York Times* bestseller list. The genesis of the book was an illustration for one of my sermons. I told a story about Honi the Circle Maker, and the Holy Spirit said in His still small voice, *That illustration is your next book*.

My first published book, *In a Pit with a Lion on a Snowy Day*, traces back to a sermon I heard when I was nineteen years old—the first time I heard the story about King David's bodyguard, Benaiah, who chased a lion into a pit on a snowy day and killed it.[2]

And the title for *All In*, believe it or not, traces back to a poker tournament I saw on ESPN.

Each book has a unique genealogy. It begins with a genesis moment—that moment when a God idea is conceived in the spirit. The revelation is taking those ideas captive with a keyboard and making them obedient to Christ. I don't type on the keyboard; I pray with it. So when I'm finished, it's not a two-hundred-page book—it's a two-hundred-page prayer. Each book I write is a unique manifestation of what God is doing in my spirit. Then I use the twenty-six letters of the English alphabet to spell out that *what if*.

Let me say it one more time.

Everything that exists was once an idea, from Noah's ark to Solomon's temple. Long before a long alphabet of animals entered the ark or Jewish pilgrims journeyed thousands of miles to Jerusalem, the ark and the temple were divine *what ifs*.

So what's *your what if*?

For some of you, it might be closer than you think. You don't have to travel halfway around the world to discover your *what if*. It could be the two-foot-tall toddler who is tugging on you, the colleague who is without Christ, or someone God has brought into your sphere of influence who needs a mentor.

Your *what if* might be a *who if*.

WHO IF

What do Billy Graham, Campus Crusade for Christ founder Bill Bright, Young Life founder Jim Rayburn, Navigators founder Dawson Trotman, and former Senate chaplain Richard Halverson have in common?

The answer is a Sunday school teacher named Henrietta Mears.

If the kingdom of God were a multilevel marketing pyramid, each of them would be Henrietta Mears's downline. Perhaps that's why *Christianity Today* dubbed her "the grandmother of us all."[3]

When Henrietta was thirty-eight years old, she moved from Minnesota to a burgeoning town called Hollywood, California. Her *what if* was the Sunday school at First Presbyterian Church in Hollywood, which Henrietta led to an astounding attendance of 6,500 students. For four decades, she faithfully devoted herself to her passion of building a cradle-to-grave Sunday school. While she was at it, she also started a publishing company called Gospel Light and a conference center called Forest Home, and she wrote a book, *What the Bible Is All About*, which has sold more than three million copies.

It's impossible to estimate how many millions of people have heard the gospel through the collective efforts of her protégés, but her kingdom influence is far greater than the six degrees of Kevin Bacon. It was her passion for Christ that fueled those pupils' fire.

Take the ministry that Bill Bright started, now called CRU. At last count, CRU had 20,000 full-time staff plus 663,000 trained volunteers in 181 countries. The ministry offshoots include Athletes in Action, Student Venture, and the Jesus Film Project. An estimated 3.4 billion people have heard the gospel through CRU.[4]

Bill Bright and his band of brothers, known as The Fellowship of the Burning Heart, shaped the twenty-first century way beyond our ability to connect the dots. Even my salvation is hyperlinked to Henrietta's influence on a young evangelist named Billy Graham. Billy Graham called her "one of the finest Christians I have ever known." It was a con-sultation with the teacher that turned into a defining moment in Billy's ministry. He walked away from that encounter with a holy confidence in Holy Scripture, and it changed the way he preached. Several decades later, the Billy Graham Association produced a film called *The Hiding Place*. And it was after watching that film that I put my faith in Christ.

Toward the end of her life, Henrietta Mears offered what could well be considered her own eulogy:

> When I get old and decrepit, I'm going to draw myself up to a television and hear my voice speak around the world. It's just wonderful to think that what we speak and do are translated some way, in a most mystical and marvelous way, to other individuals and they in turn spread it out and out and out until the circle is so immense that we haven't any idea.[5]

You may not influence millions of people, but you may influence one person who influences millions. You might be parenting or coaching or teaching or mentoring or employing the next Henrietta Mears, the next Billy Graham, the next Bill Bright. Whatever they accomplish for the kingdom of God is part of your spiritual downline!

At the very end of his letter to the Romans, Paul shares his *who's who* list. There are twenty-nine names—Paul's upline and downline.

Who's on your Romans 16 list?

Who's your *who if*?

My greatest legacy is not the church I pastor or the books I write. My greatest legacy is our three children. They are my *who if*. While no parent should take all of the credit or all of the blame for who their children become, children are a manifestation of their family of origin. They are the time capsules we send to the next generation. And there is no more important *what if* than the *who ifs* God entrusts to us as parents.

3

Bold Predictions

The 1932 World Series between the Chicago Cubs and the New York Yankees was tied, one win apiece. Game three was tied, four runs to four. That's when, in the top of the fourth inning, Babe Ruth stepped into the batter's box.

It was a classic showdown between baseball icons. Charlie Root was, and still is, the winningest pitcher in Chicago Cubs history. Babe Ruth was, well, The Babe. Ruth took strike one from the right-hander. When he took strike two, the fans at Wrigley Field started heckling him. That's when Babe Ruth stepped out of the batter's box and pointed his bat to center field. Then he hit the next pitch 440 feet to the place where he pointed. The Babe called his shot.

That home run won game three, and the Yankees went on to win the 1932 World Series. Like many legends, this one has taken on a life of its own over the years. But legends are born of bold predictions, and it's those bold predictions that change the course of history.

On May 25, 1961, John F. Kennedy stood before a joint session of Congress at a critical juncture in the space race. The Soviet Union had launched Sputnik into Earth's orbit a few years before. They had a significant head start, but President Kennedy confidently declared that we'd win the space race. In his inimitable Bostonian accent, he said, "I believe that this nation should commit itself to achieving the goal, before this decade is out, of landing a man on the moon and returning him safely to the Earth."[1]

JFK's *what if* became reality on July 20, 1969, the day Neil Armstrong took one small step for man, one giant leap for mankind.

If history turns on a dime, the dime is bold predictions. They've got to be backed up with bold actions. And if it's the space race, some cold hard cash too. But it starts by pointing a bat toward center field. It starts by making a speech, setting a deadline, and then backing it up with a $531 million budget.

What if starts with bold predictions.

It's Martin Luther posting ninety-five theses on the doors of the Castle Church in Wittenberg, Germany, on October 31, 1517.

It's Dr. Martin Luther King Jr. delivering his "I Have a Dream" speech on the steps of the Lincoln Memorial on August 28, 1963.

In my case, it was vowing to write my first book by my thirty-fifth birthday. That's not as epic as the history-changing moments I've referenced, but it was a game changer for me. It was one of my *what if* moments.

SMALL BEGINNINGS

I felt called to write as a twenty-two-year-old seminary student, but I didn't self-publish my first book until thirteen years later. Dreams without deadlines usually turn into *if only* regrets. I had half a dozen half-finished manuscripts on my computer, but I couldn't tie off the umbilical cord. As the years passed, I stopped celebrating my birthday and started despising it. My birthday became an annual reminder of a dream deferred. Writing books was my *what if*, but all I had to show for it was *if only*.

I'm not sure where the idea came from, but I decided to throw down the gauntlet. I made a bold prediction forty days before my thirty-fifth birthday, vowing that I wouldn't turn thirty-five without a book to show for it. It would be my gift to myself, and somehow I pulled it off. It's certainly not my best-written book, and I had to foot the bill to self-publish it. But I proved to myself that I could do it.

I made another bold prediction when I was twenty-two. I had totally forgotten all about it until Lora recently reminded me of it. When I felt called to write, I didn't just tell Lora that I was going to write a book. I told her I was going to write a book that sold a million copies.

Knowing what I know now, it sounds a little naïve. After all, 97 percent of books don't sell five thousand copies total. What makes it even crazier is that I had just taken an occupational assessment revealing a low aptitude for writing. But I fanned into flame the gift of God by reading thousands of books before I wrote one. I honed my skills by manuscripting sermons and writing blog posts. Finally, I self-published *ID: The True You*. It only sold 3,641 copies, a far cry from one million. My first royalty? $110.43. But that bold prediction was fulfilled when my sixth book, *The Circle Maker*, became my first book to cross the million-sold mark.

What bold prediction do you need to make?

Maybe it's time to throw down the gauntlet. Pray a bold prayer! Dream a God-sized dream. After all, if you are big enough for your dream, your dream isn't big enough for God.

But one word of caution. You can't just make a bold prediction, then sit back and hope it happens. No matter how big your dream is, you have to prove yourself faithful with a few things. But if you do little things like they're big things, then God will do big things like they are little things!

·I believe that you are destined, predestined. But don't turn it into a theological crutch or an excuse for less effort. I want to hear God say, "Well done, good and faithful servant."[2] I want an A for effort. God is setting up divine appointments, but you have to keep them. God is the gift giver, but you have to fan them into flame. God is calling, but you have to answer. God is ordering your footsteps, but you have to keep in step with the Spirit. And God is preparing good works in advance, but you need to carpe diem.

It doesn't matter whether it's sports history, space race history, or your history—it's bold predictions backed up by bold actions that change history. And no one made bolder predictions than the Ancient of Days. He didn't just predict who would betray Him, how He would be tortured, His method of execution, or His resurrection, right down to the day—He made some bold predictions about your life!

WORLD FAMOUS

Everybody needs somebody who believes in them more than they themselves do. One of those people in my life has been Bob Rhoden.

Even though we started out with a core group of only nineteen people at National Community Church, I was still underqualified because I had zero experience. The only thing on my résumé was a summer internship at my home church, and all I did was manage the men's softball league. Well, I guess there was a failed church plant too. But that wasn't an asset; it was a liability.

Still, Bob Rhoden saw something in me that I didn't see in myself. A decade later, he invited me to join him as a trustee of a charitable foundation. I don't get it, but I'm grateful. What a joy and privilege giving grants to kingdom causes is! We get to make other people's *what ifs* happen.

One of the most important and most underrated skill sets of a Christ follower is the ability to spot potential. It doesn't matter whether you're a GM on draft day, making a political appointment, or coaching Little League. Few things will shape your future more than the ability to see possibilities where others see impossibilities—it's called faith.

No one was better at this than Jesus. He wasn't afraid to put self-righteous people in their place with a well-worded rebuke. He once said to Peter, "Get behind me, Satan!"[3] But long before that He also saw *Peter* in Simon. Then He turned an ordinary fisherman into a fisher of men.

The prediction no one saw coming involved a prostitute. Even the disciples gave her a hard time when she anointed Jesus. But Jesus made his boldest prediction yet:

> Truly I tell you, wherever this gospel is preached throughout the world, what she has done will also be told, in memory of her.[4]

If you interpret this literally—and I do—this ranks as one of the most amazing predictions in the Bible! Come on, what are the chances? There were seventy-seven Roman Caesars, and you can't name five of them unless you majored in ancient Roman history or watch way too much *Jeopardy!* There were 332 pharaohs, and the only one you can name is King Tut or the one in *Night at the Museum.*

The who's who of history are long forgotten. No matter how famous these figures may have been, only a select few are remembered a hundred years later. So what are the chances of a Jewish prostitute being remembered two thousand years later? I'd say slim and none, and slim just left town.

Even fifteen minutes of fame seems unlikely, but here we are two thousand years removed, and you're reading about her right now. If this book follows the same path as others, you're reading about her in dozens of languages, all around the world. And each time her story is read, that bold prediction is fulfilled one more time!

It's never too late to become who you might have been.

It was true for this prostitute.

And it's true for you.

God has made some bold predictions about you—they're called *promises*. There are thousands of them, and you can take each one to the bank. Why? Because the One who made those promises always delivers. The resurrection is the down payment on every promise. If God made good on that prediction, what are you worried about?

God does not overpromise or underdeliver.

If we meet the conditions, He always exceeds expectations.

4

I Dwell in Possibility

If God is for us, who can be against us?

Romans 8:31

On any given day, 23,000 scheduled flights take off and land at American airports.[1] At any given time, 5,000 of those airplanes are simultaneously airborne. That means that approximately one million people are flying 300 mph at 30,000 feet at any given moment. Kind of crazy to think about, isn't it? A hundred years ago, this was the stuff of science fiction. Then two brothers, Wilbur and Orville, turned science fiction into science fact.

As you can probably guess by now, it all started with *what if*.

The Wright brothers' dream of flying traces back to an autumn day in 1878 when their father, Bishop Milton Wright, brought home a rather unique toy. Using a rubber band to twirl its rotor, a miniature bamboo helicopter flew into the air. Much like our mechanized toy helicopters, it broke after a few flights. But instead of giving up on it and going on to the next toy, the Wright brothers made their own. And the dream of flying was conceived.

A quarter century later, on December 17, 1903, Orville himself went airborne for twelve gravity-defying seconds in the first powered, piloted flight in history.

It's almost impossible to imagine life as we know it without airplanes. But like every innovation, every revolution, every breakthrough, someone had to imagine the impossible first.

Every dream has a genesis moment—a moment when *possibility* pulls off a coup d'état and overthrows impossibility. It usually starts small—as small as a toy helicopter. It takes time and patience for the genesis to become revelation. But the chain reaction of faith defies gravity, defies the imagination. Without knowing it, the Wright brothers were creating the airline industry, the FAA, and the TSA. I'm sure it never crossed their minds, but their flying faith is the reason why a million people are speeding through the troposphere right now.

The next time you take off in a Boeing 747, remember that it's *what if* that enables our dreams to take off. It was two pastor's kids, Wilbur and Orville, who punched your ticket with their possibility thinking.

POSSIBILITY

A decade after the Wright brothers took flight at Kitty Hawk, a young nurse's aide in Toronto was caring for dying soldiers returning from the warfront. During breaks, Amelia took her mind off the grave circumstances by watching planes take off at a nearby airfield.

On a snowy day in 1918, the backwash from an airplane's propellers threw freezing snow into her face. It woke her up to *what if.* "It was the finest cold shower ever imagined," she later reflected. "I determined then and there that I would someday ride one of these devil machines, and make it blow snow to my will."[2]

Amelia Earhart did just that, becoming the first woman to fly solo across the Atlantic Ocean. She died just a few time zones short of her dream of flying around the world, but not before inspiring a generation of women to pursue their *what ifs.*

A century before Earhart's trip around the world, an introverted poet named Emily Dickinson took flight with words. Fewer than a dozen of her 1,800 poems were published during her lifetime, but one of them ranks as my all-time favorite: "I Dwell in Possibility."

That title encapsulates my personality.

According to the StrengthsFinder assessment, my top five strengths are Strategic, Learner, Futuristic, Ideation, and Self-Assurance. Those talents combine into one StrengthsFinder label: trailblazer. Simply put, I see possibility behind every bush—every bush is a burning bush where God might show up and show off His glory!

That combination of characteristics is perfectly captured by Dickinson's one-liner: I dwell in possibility. I love it so much that I have an artist's rendering of those four words, *I dwell in possibility*, prominently displayed in my office. I've even named my office after Dickinson's poem. Hey, people name boats. Why not offices? So when you walk into my office, you walk into *Possibility*.

It's not just where I go to work; it's where I dream of ways to change the world. I'm a possibility thinker. Is there a downside to that type of personality? Undoubtedly! For starters, I'm easily bored. If it's not challenging, I check out.

The upside is that I have an eye for opportunity. In fact, I see opportunity everywhere I look. I'm like Dug, the talking dog in the Pixar classic *Up*. Every time he sees a squirrel he says, "Squirrel!" and his attention is

100 percent diverted from whatever it was on. In my case, the squirrel is named *opportunity*.

I think it's why *if* is my first instinct and *what if* is second nature. *If* is the way I'm wired, but no matter what your personality type, I believe it's a biblical imperative. *If* God is for us, then *what if* isn't optional. My prayer is Søren Kierkegaard's plea:

> If I were to wish for anything I should not wish for wealth and power, but for the passionate sense of what can be, for the eye which, ever young and ardent, sees the possible. Pleasure disappoints, possibility never. And what wine is so sparkling, what so fragrant, what so intoxicating as possibility?[3]

WE PUT A MAN ON THE MOON

I recently did a chapel for the Green Bay Packers. I've done quite a few NFL chapels, but it's a little different doing a chapel for the team you pulled for, yea even prayed for, as a kid. In fact, I used to cry when they lost, which was quite often in my formative years!

I'm not sure my message had anything to do with it, but the Packers put up 42 points in the first half of that game! And we had front row seats for the Lambeau Leaps! A friend texted me during the game, "You're living the dream right now, aren't you?" That's when it dawned on me, *yes, yes I am!* It was one of those "pinch me" moments.

The day of the game, I spent some time with the team's chaplain and pastor of Green Bay Community Church, Troy Murphy. He gave me the nickel tour of their building, and I picked up a very cool idea. Hanging outside every team member's office was a sign revealing their personality profile and strengths.

The cheat sheets also listed dos and don'ts, followed by a one-liner. I loved the "don't" on Troy's sign: "Don't say I can't." We must be cut from the same cloth. When someone tells me why something can't be done, it drives me crazy! I usually remind them that we put a man on the moon. So don't tell me it can't be done!

All things are possible.

Nothing is impossible.

That covers all bases, doesn't it? But just for good measure, we can do all things through Christ who strengthens us![4] To an infinite God, all finites are equal. That's the essence of *what if*.

Where others see problems, *what if* sees solutions.

Where others see impossibility, *what if* sees opportunity.

IT ALL STARTS WITH *IF*

During the first-ever college football National Championship Game with the playoff format, the Ohio

State Buckeyes faced off against the Oregon Ducks. The Buckeyes won the game, but the Ducks won the commercial. No offense, but the Buckeyes commercial was absolutely forgettable.

The Ducks commercial was as unique as their uniforms. Here's a remix of that spot, "Explore the Power of 'If.'" The spot began by asking: "What if there was no *if*?"[5]

Deep in the woods, *if* sparks a revolution. . . .
If searches and researches. . . .
If opens doors. . . .
Goes for it on fourth down.
If doesn't care about yesterday. . . .
Just two simple letters, right?
Wrong.
If sleeps never. And goes for extra credit. . . .
It all starts with *if*.
Because *if* becomes *when*, and when becomes *now*.
And now becomes *how*, and how becomes . . .
wow.
If will change your stance.
If will change the game.
If will change the world.[6]

Their tackling could have been better, but not their tagline: "We *if* at the University of Oregon." Bravo,

Oregon, bravo! Maybe it's because I'm an *if* fanatic, but that ad is pure brilliance.

When it comes to *if*, my point of reference is Romans 8:31. It's where possibility is conceived. It's where opportunity is perceived. And it always starts with God. If God is with you, for you—it's game on, it's game over.

In the beginning, God created us in His image. And we've been creating God in our image ever since! The technical term is *anthropomorphism*. What you end up with is an idol that is a mirror image of yourself. In the words of A. W. Tozer, "a God who can never surprise us, never overwhelm us, nor astonish us, nor transcend us."[7]

That's not the God I believe in.

That's not the God of the Bible.

I believe in a God who is omnipotent, omniscient, and omnipresent. I believe in a God who is high and exalted. I believe in a God who is able to do immeasurably more than all I can ask or imagine.[8] I believe in a God whose thoughts are higher than my thoughts, whose ways are higher than my ways.[9] I believe in a God whose love I can't possibly comprehend, whose power I can't possibly control, whose mercy I can't possibly deserve. I believe in the God who exists outside of the four dimensions of space-time He created. I believe in the God who can make and break the laws of nature.

His name is Wonderful Counselor, the Mighty God, the Everlasting Father, and the Prince of Peace. And He shall reign forever and ever![10]

"How much happier you would be, how much more of you there would be," said G. K. Chesterton, "if the hammer of a higher God could smash your small cosmos."[11]

God is able.

That is the first and last tenet of my theology—my a priori assumption, my fallback position, my default setting.

5

Change Agents

On August 26, 1910, Anjezë Gonxhe Bojaxhiu was born in Skopje, Albania. And you thought it was hard learning to spell your name! At the age of seventeen, Anjezë devoted her life to God's service while praying at the shrine to the Black Madonna.

After joining the Sisters of Loreta, Anjezë was first stationed at Loreto Abbey in Rathfarnham, Ireland. After taking her religious vows as a nun, she chose to be named after Thérèse de Lisieux, the patron saint of missionaries. We know her as Mother Teresa.

Shortly after taking her vows, she shared her *what if* with her mother superiors. "I have three pennies and a dream from God to build an orphanage."

Her superiors said, "You can't build an orphanage with three pennies. With three pennies you can't do anything."

Mother Teresa smiled and said, "I know. But with God and three pennies I can do anything."[1]

For fifty years, Anjezë worked among the poorest of the poor in the slums of Calcutta, India. In 1979, she won the Nobel Peace Prize. And nearly two decades after her death, the ministry she started, Missionaries of Charity, consists of 4,500 sisters serving in 133 countries.

How does such a "little flower," the meaning of her birth name, become one of the most recognizable and revered women in the world? How does a woman with three pennies inspire billions of dollars given to charity?

The answer is *what if*.

Never underestimate someone with a God-given *if*.

CHANGE AGENTS

A few years ago, a handful of Colombian farmers cut down their cocaine fields in a guerilla conflict zone after hearing the gospel. They risked their lives and their livelihood to grow coffee beans instead of coca plants.

Santiago Moncada, a native of Colombia, saw an opportunity to come alongside the good work God had already begun. Santi brought back five pounds of coffee beans and a dream called Redeeming Grounds. As with any dream, it took some financial equity and some sweat equity.

But that dream is now a reality because Santi had the courage to ask *what if*. Ebenezer's coffeehouse has partnered with Redeeming Grounds, selling 285 bags year-to-date. This year they'll purchase 16,000 pounds of coffee beans. I don't think Starbucks needs to worry just yet. But even the biggest of dreams has small beginnings.

And if you don't despise the day of small beginnings, the God who began a good work will carry it to completion. Why? Because it's not your vision; it's His. It's not your business; it's His. It's not your job; it's His. It's not your cause; it's His.

Someone may have hired you to do your job, but make no mistake about it, they didn't call you. Only God can call us. You may have been elected to your position, but make no mistake about it, your constituents didn't call you; God did. No matter where you work or what you do, you are called by God.

Your job is your sermon.

Your colleagues are your congregation.

That sense of calling turns Monday morning into *what if*.

The mission arm of National Community Church is called A18, as in Acts 1:8. During our annual missions series this year, we used latitude and longitude coordinates as the series theme because we wanted to remind our congregation that no matter where you are, you are *on mission*. We'll take thirty-four mission trips this year, but you don't have to go halfway around the world to be on mission.

That's why we had seven NCCers from seven domains of society share TED-style talks about how they leverage their jobs into callings.[2]

Erica Symonette is a self-proclaimed fashionista. She has leveraged her passion for fashion into an online store called *Pulchritude*. "The world doesn't need another boutique," Erica admitted. "But it does need more kingdom businesses." Her store is a manifestation of Isaiah 61:10: "he has clothed you with garments of salvation." Erica uses net profits to help victims of sex trafficking.[3]

Joshua DuBois feels called to the political arena. He is the former head of the Office of Faith-Based and Neighborhood Partnerships in the executive office of the White House, but even if you report to the president, you still answer to a higher authority! "I went to policy school, not seminary," Joshua said. Yet for seven years, he functioned as a prophet to the president, sharing a daily word of encouragement with POTUS.

Kate Schmidgall was voted Young Entrepreneur of the Year by the DC Chamber of Council in 2013.

Her design firm, Bittersweet, turns stats into stories, awareness into action. Kate unapologetically says, "Nonprofits are *for* profit." If you don't make a profit, the business model isn't sustainable. The difference? Bittersweet uses those net profits to cast a net for kingdom purposes.[4]

Finally, Shajena Erazo teaches at one of DC's toughest public schools. Her high school has a history of making the news for all the wrong reasons. No matter how many security guards or metal detectors they put in place, they couldn't seem to keep crime out. That school is Sha's mission field. "I see myself as a youth pastor," she says. "I just don't report to church. I report to my principal." Sha is every bit as called to teach high school English as I am to preach the gospel. After reading *The Circle Maker*, she started circling her high school. Sha anoints students' desks with oil; she prays with fellow teachers; and by the end of every school year, her journal is filled with pages of prayers for each of her students.

In their own unique way, each of these change agents is asking *what if*. They refuse to be paralyzed by statistics. They are making a difference one person, one project, one class at a time. They know God has called them and has anointed them.

It doesn't matter what domain of society you work in or where you are on the org chart. You are called and commissioned by God. You are right where God wants you to be—even if you're not where *you* want to be. Sometimes the greatest sermon is doing a good job at a bad job or doing a thankless job with a grateful heart.

On Mission

I have a few convictions when it comes to calling. They are keys to unlocking *what if*.

First, God doesn't call the qualified. He qualifies the called.

There is a high likelihood that God will call you to do something you're not smart enough, good enough, or strong enough to pull off. By definition, a God-ordained dream will always be beyond your ability and beyond your resources. Why? So that you have to rely on God every single day!

I'm keenly aware of the fact that in my current state of spiritual maturity, I'm not capable of leading National Community Church two years from now. I need to keep growing, keep learning. And that's the way it should be. Nothing keeps you on your knees in raw dependence upon God like a God-sized dream.

Second, criticize by creating.

In my opinion, criticism is a cop-out for those who are too lazy to solve the problem they are complaining about. Instead of criticizing movies or music, produce a film or an album that is better than whatever it is you're complaining about. The most constructive criticism is called creativity.

At the end of the day, we should be more known for what we're *for* than what we're *against*. Anybody can point out problems. We're called to solve them by writing better books, starting better schools, and drafting better legislation.

Third, the anointing is for everyone.

It doesn't matter whether you're a teacher, a doctor, a lawyer, or a barista. From the top of the organization chart to the bottom, God wants to anoint you to do whatever it is you're called to do.

If I need surgery, I certainly want a doctor who has been to med school. But I want more than that: I want a doctor whose hands are anointed by God.

Fourth, live for the applause of nail-scarred hands.

Whatever it is that you feel called to do, do it as if your life depended on it. That's 1 Corinthians 10:31 in a nutshell: "So whether you eat or drink or whatever you do, do it all for the glory of God."

The key word is *whatever*. It doesn't matter what you're doing; do it to the glory of God. "It is inbred in us that we have to do exceptional things for God," said Oswald Chambers, "but we have not. We have to be exceptional in the ordinary things."[5] And when we are, we put a smile on God's face.

MUNDANE TASKS

Richard Bolles, author of the classic bestseller *What Color Is Your Parachute?*, makes a profound observation: "The story in the Gospels of Jesus going up on the mount and being transfigured before the disciples is to me a picture of what calling is all about. Taking the mundane, offering it to God, and asking Him to transfigure it."[6]

Taking mundane tasks and figuring out how to transfigure them.

That's what *what if* is all about.

More than a decade ago, I gave the eulogy at a memorial service in the Caucus Room of the Russell Senate Office Building. Some of the most important hearings in our nation's history have been held in that room. If those walls could talk!

Yet here we were to honor the life of a woman with no rank. Jayonna Beal was the administrative assistant in charge of constituent correspondence for fourteen years. That isn't the position people are fighting for on the hill, but Jayonna did it with grace. She didn't have position or power, but that room was packed with the who's who of Washington.

I spoke right after her boss, who would run for president a few years later. He, along with countless others, shared stories of how Jayonna's small acts of kindness made a big difference in their lives. Jayonna baked cookies, sewed buttons, and showed interns the ropes. And she did it all in the name of Jesus. Jayonna practiced that old adage, "Share the gospel every day; if necessary, use words."

It's the little *ifs* that change the world.

In the words of Dr. Martin Luther King Jr.,

> If a man is called to be a street sweeper, he should sweep streets even as Michelangelo painted, or Beethoven composed music, or Shakespeare wrote poetry. He should sweep streets so well that all the hosts of heaven will pause to say, "Here lived a great street sweeper who did his job well."[7]

I know a great street sweeper. Her name is Val, and she is a custodian who cleans like it's nobody's business but God's. She inscribed *SDG* on her mop handle, just like Johann Sebastian Bach did on his symphonies. It stands for *Soli Deo Gloria*. It's a reminder that she cleans for the glory of God.

Believe it or not, Val drove all the way from Canada to clean our offices at National Community Church. I know that sounds strange, but I think it falls into the category of *strange and mysterious*. She was profoundly impacted by our podcast, and she wanted to repay her debt of gratitude the best way she knew how. So she drove all the way to DC to clean our offices.

Who does that?

I'll tell you who. Someone who knows God has called them. Back home, Val is the custodian for the school district. It's often a thankless job, the job no one else wants to do. And it isn't always easy. "My prayer last year was that God would get me off the third shift," Val told me. "But now I have changed my prayers. I want to be taught by God what I need to learn."

There might be educators in her district smarter than her, but I dare say that no one is more teachable than the custodian. And that's what really counts in God's kingdom.

Being a third-shift custodian isn't most people's dream job. But *what* you do isn't as important as *how* you do it and *whom* you do it for. So no matter what you do, do it like Michelangelo painted, Beethoven composed, Shakespeare wrote poetry, and Val cleans bathrooms.

Whatever you do, don't settle for *what*.

Imagine *what if*.

6

One Last *If*

I was seated in the Grand Ballroom of the Washington Hilton hotel on February 2, 2012, along with 3,500 of my closest friends.

Since 1953, the National Prayer Breakfast has been a fixture on the first Thursday of February. The guest list includes ambassadors, diplomats, and heads of state from a hundred countries. The guest of honor is the president of the United States.

Then there are the average joes, like me. To be honest, the pomp and circumstance is a little distracting. I was more focused on figuring out who was who than listening to what was being said from the stage. Then that year's keynote speaker, Eric Metaxas, said something that resulted in a eureka moment. I'm not sure why it struck me the way it did, when it did. But one sentence struck a dominant seventh chord.

He said, "Everything I rejected about God was not God."[1]

It was like tectonic plates shifted with that one seismic statement, and I still feel the aftershocks. Most people who reject God are really rejecting religion, without knowing it. They aren't really rejecting God for who He *is*. They are actually rejecting God for who He *isn't*.

Eric pushed the envelope even further: "Everything I rejected about God was not God. It was religion. It was people who go to church and do not show the love of Jesus, people who don't practice what they preach, people who are indifferent to the poor and suffering. I had rejected that, but guess what? Jesus had also rejected that. Jesus was and is the enemy of dead religion."

Let me pull that thread.

The most insidious lie we can believe about God is that He is somehow *against* us. It's the very same lie that planted seeds of doubt in Eve's spirit in the Garden of Eden.

We've doubted God's goodness ever since, and it's the root cause of a thousand other problems. If the enemy can get us to buy into that original lie, we posture ourselves against God because we think God is against us. Then we reject God for all the wrong reasons.

No. No. A thousand times no!

God is *for* you.

God is *for* you in every way imaginable.

God is *for* you for all eternity.

There is a simple rule of thumb in journalism: don't bury the lead. So here's the lead: *God is for you*.

Back to Eric Metaxas.

Along with identifying what he'd rejected that wasn't really God, he profiled the good God he had rediscovered by seeking Him from a place of honesty rather than religiosity. He detailed God's most applaudable attributes, and then he asked a brilliant question: "Who would reject that?"[2]

It was a rhetorical question, but let me answer it anyway. The obvious answer is, no one! No one would reject a God like that.

I have a theory: *If you don't love God, it's because you don't know God.*

I hope that doesn't come across as condescending in any way, shape, or form. I just believe it. *To know God is to love God.* Not the God who *isn't*; the God who *is*.

What is there to not love? After all, God *is* love. Those who reject God because they believe God is *against* them are rejecting who God *isn't*.

THE LAW OF THE LEVER

Archimedes of Syracuse is famous for jumping out of his bathtub, running naked through the streets, and yelling, "Eureka!" after discovering the principle of water displacement. That is likely an ancient urban legend, but Archimedes certainly ranks as one of the most brilliant minds in antiquity. In the second century BC, he came very close to pinpointing the value of pi, showing it to be greater than $\frac{223}{71}$ and less than $\frac{22}{7}$.

The world's first seagoing steamship with a screw propeller was the SS *Archimedes*, named in honor of Archimedes' screw pump. He even has a moon crater, a lunar mountain range, and an asteroid, *3600 Archimedes*, named in honor of his astronomical achievements. But he is perhaps most famous for one oft-quoted quip: "Give me a place to stand, and I will move the earth."[3]

Archimedes didn't invent the lever, but he did coin the law of the lever. Simply put, a lever amplifies input force to provide greater output force. The longer the lever, the greater the leverage.

The concept of leverage has been, well, leveraged in a thousand ways. But let me zero in on systems thinking. In any system, a leverage point is the place in a system's structure where a solution element can be applied. A high leverage point is a place where *a small amount of change force can cause a large change in the system's behavior.* It's a 1 percent change that makes a 99 percent difference.

There is no higher leverage point than the two-letter word *if*.

It defines our deepest regrets: *if only.*

It defies impossible circumstances: *as if.*

It's pregnant with infinite possibilities: *what if.*

And it overcomes all refutations: no *ifs, ands, or buts* about it.

Biblically speaking, *if* is the conditional conjunction that turns God's eternal promises into our present realities. Each of those promises is a high leverage point, but perhaps no promise in the Bible has more leverage than Romans 8:31:

> If God is for us, who can be against us?

God is for you.

The question is, are you for God?

ONE LAST IF

> If you confess with your mouth, Jesus is Lord, and believe in your heart that God raised him from the dead, you shall be saved.[4]

You are one *if* away from salvation.

The moment you put your faith in Jesus Christ, everything changes forever. Not only is your sin forgiven and forgotten, but the righteousness of Christ is credited to your account. The heavenly Father signs your adoption papers. Your name is written in the Lamb's book of life.

When you make a confession of faith in Christ, it's the end of *if only* and the beginning of *what if.* That one *if* unlocks every promise in Scripture. That one *if* is the beginning of happily *forever* after.

Why not make that decision right here, right now? One last *if.*

When John Bruce, a federal judge appointed by Ulysses S. Grant, was on his deathbed, he instructed his daughter to "Fetch the book."[5] He told her to turn to the eighth chapter of Romans in his well-read, well-lived Bible. Then he said, "Put my finger on these words," and quoted its last promise:

> For I am persuaded, that neither death, nor
>   life, nor angels, nor principalities, nor
>   powers, nor things present, nor things to
>   come,
> Nor height, nor depth, nor any other creature,
>   shall be able to separate us from the love of
>   God, which is in Christ Jesus our Lord.[6]

When his daughter found those words, John Bruce told her to hold his finger there. He passed away with his finger on that promise. What a way to enter heaven, the eternal *what if*. My advice, at the end of this little book, is to fetch *that* Book. Put your finger on its promises!

In time, your *if only* regrets will fade to black.

In eternity, your *what if* dreams will come to light.

No if, ands, or buts about it.

Notes

Chapter 1 The Power of *If*

1. Howard Schultz and Dori Jones Yang, *Pour Your Heart into It: How Starbucks Built a Company One Cup at a Time* (New York: Hyperion, 1997), 63.

2. "Starbucks Coffee: How Many Cups of Coffee Does Starbucks Sell Each Year?" Quora query answered by Ali Ahmed, January 17, 2011, http://www.quora.com/Starbucks-Coffee-How-many-cups-of-coffee-does-Starbucks-sell-each-year. Accessed March 18, 2015.

3. "15 Facts about Starbucks That Will Blow Your Mind," Business Insider, http://www.businessinsider.com/15-facts-about-starbucks-that-will-blow-your-mind-2011-3?op=1#ixzz3Uki21JWv. Accessed March 18, 2015.

4. Robert Cowley, *What If?* (New York: Putnam, 1999), xi.

Chapter 2 Who If

1. Psalm 139:13–16.

2. See 1 Chronicles 11.

3. W. M. Zoba, "The Grandmother of Us All," *Christianity Today* 40, no. 10 (September 16, 1996), 44–46.

4. Marcus Brotherton, *"Teacher": The Henrietta Mears Story* (Ventura, CA: Regal, 2012), 10.

5. Ibid., 145.

Chapter 3 Bold Predictions

1. President John F. Kennedy, "Special Message to the Congress on Urgent National Needs," May 25, 1961, excerpt quoted at NASA.gov, https://www.nasa.gov/vision/space/features/jfk_speech_text.html. Accessed March 25, 2015.

2. Matthew 25:21.

3. Matthew 16:23.

4. Matthew 26:13.

Chapter 4 I Dwell in Possibility

1. Matthew Alice, "On an Average Day, How Many Airplanes Are in the Sky across the United States?" Straight from the Hip, *San Diego Reader*, May 17, 2001, http://www.sandiegoreader.com/news/2001/may/17/average-day-how-many-airplanes-are-sky-across-unit/#. Accessed March 26, 2015.

2. "Exploring History," *National Geographic* (Winter 2012), 21.

3. Søren Kierkegaard, *Either/Or: A Fragment of Life* (New York: Penguin Classics, 1992), 14.

4. See Philippians 4:13.

5. University of Oregon, "Explore the Power of 'If,'" YouTube video, posted January 1, 2015, https://www.youtube.com/watch?v=6fvPsoidQmI.

6. Ibid.

7. A. W. Tozer, "God of Glory" (devotional), The Alliance, October 31, 2012, https://www.cmalliance.org/devotions/tozer?id=1346, accessed April 17, 2015.

8. See Ephesians 3:20.

9. See Isaiah 55:8.

10. See Isaiah 9:6–7.

11. G. K. Chesterton, *Orthodoxy* (Ortho Publishing, 2014), 13.

Chapter 5 Change Agents

1. Quoted in Jack Canfield and Mark Victor Hansen, *The Aladdin Factor* (New York: Berkley Books, 1995), 255.

2. Videos of these stories are available online: "A18: Innovate," National Community Church, November 23, 2014, http://theaterchurch.com/media/a18/aoneeight-innovate.

3. See www.shoppulchritude.com.

4. See www.bittersweetmonthly.com.

5. Oswald Chambers, "Direction by Impulse," *My Utmost for His Highest*, online daily devotional, October 21, 2014, http://utmost.org /classic/direction-by-impulse-classic/.

6. Quoted in John Maxwell, *Life@Work: Marketplace Success for People of Faith* (Nashville: Thomas Nelson, 2005), 127.

7. Dr. Martin Luther King Jr., quoted at The King Center online, "Quote of the Week," April 9, 2013, http://www.thekingcenter.org /blog/mlk-quote-week-all-labor-uplifts-humanity-has-dignity-and-im portance-and-should-be-undertaken.

Chapter 6 One Last *If*

1. "National Prayer Breakfast," CSPAN transcript, February 2, 2012, http://www.c-span.org/video/?304149-1/national-prayer-breakfast.

2. Ibid.

3. See "The Lever: Introduction," http://www.math.nyu.edu/~cr orres/Archimedes/Lever/LeverIntro.html. Accessed March 18, 2015.

4. Romans 10:9–10.

5. See F. W. Boreham, *Life Verses* (Grand Rapids: Kregel, 1994), 226.

6. Romans 8:38–39 KJV.

Mark Batterson is the *New York Times* bestselling author of *The Circle Maker*, *The Grave Robber*, and *A Trip around the Sun*. He is the lead pastor of National Community Church, one church with seven campuses in Washington, DC. Mark has a doctor of ministry degree from Regent University and lives on Capitol Hill with his wife, Lora, and their three children. Learn more at www.markbatterson.com.

Connect with

MARK
BATTERSON
at
MarkBatterson.com

@MarkBatterson

Mark Batterson

@MarkBatterson

Connect with National Community Church at
WWW.THEATERCHURCH.COM

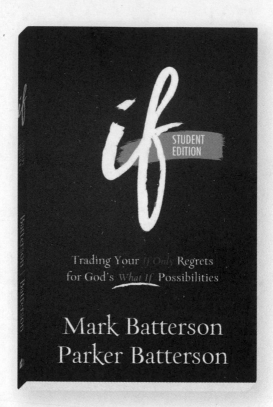